BIRD IMPRESSIONS

BIRD IMPRESSIONS

A personal view of birds

DARREN REES

SWAN·HILL
PRESS

FOR GWYNNETH

Copyright © Darren Rees 1993

First published in the UK in 1993
by Swan Hill Press
an imprint of Airlife Publishing Ltd

British Cataloguing in Publication Data
 A catalogue record for this book
 is available from the British Library

ISBN 1 85310 286 5

Printed by Stige, Turin, Italy

Swan Hill Press
an imprint of Airlife Publishing Ltd.
101 Longden Road, Shrewsbury SY3 9EB, England

Eider – End of Day Study   1988

FOREWORD

To watch the work of a young artist develop and mature is a rewarding experience. I have known Darren Rees for thirteen years and have enjoyed seeing his style evolve. Like all the best wildlife artists, his work is largely based on direct observation from life. It is a privilege to be allowed to look through his sketch books where he has caught the movement, the fleeting observation, in quick confident lines, or made more studied drawings when his subject allowed. The best of his paintings draw on the immediate experience in the field and this book is full of such work. Most of the pictures come from his period in Wales, and his words vividly recall the occasions that inspired them.

Darren has studied with equal care the places where his birds are to be seen, the textures of the rocks and plants and the ever-changing surface of water.

His pictures, whether a wide view or a concentration on a small piece of habitat, carry a conviction which comes from that intense observation. He is particularly successful when drawing birds in flight, capturing the effortless gliding of kites or the lively, bouyant aerobatics of choughs.

While absorbing influences from the work of artists he admires, Darren has developed his personal handling of that most difficult of mediums, watercolour; his own immediately recognisable style has a delightful freedom of expression, without being over-loose or uncontrolled. The flicks of his brush accurately convey the appearance of vegetation without the deadening overworking that is sadly typical of much work in this genre.

Darren Rees is one of those artists who, in his approach to wildlife art, seek to capture the character of the animal, its "jizz", rather than to present a detailed scientific study. In this way he helps us to see the life in the bird far more successfully than many formal and so-called "photographic" portraits.

I first came to know Darren's work well in 1981, as one of the judges of the Bird Illustrator of the Year Awards, when we selected him for the Richard Richardson Award for artists aged under 21. This competition, organised by the monthly Journal *British Birds*, has provided many aspiring bird artists with their first step on the ladder. Darren went on to gain third and second places in the senior competition and, in 1989, he won the PJC Award for an individual drawing of outstanding merit.

In 1985 he was elected to membership of the Society of Wildlife Artists, a signal honour for one so young, and in the same year received the first RSPB Fine Art Award, for a picture selected from the Society's annual exhibition. He also won the inaugural Natural World Art Award in 1987 for the painting of *Sandwich Terns,* which I am glad to find included here.

In 1984 he made the brave decision to leave a secure teaching post and become a freelance wildlife artist. This enabled him to take a part-time post in 1986 with the RSPB at their Welsh headquarters in Powys, giving him plenty of opportunities to study birds at first hand and to illustrate a wide range of publications. The disciplines of producing artwork to order were invaluable to his progress as an artist.

Although Darren has provided fine illustrations in colour and black and white for several books, this is the first which is all his own. *Bird Impressions* launched a fully-rounded talent which has fulfilled that early promise. It is a major milestone on what I feel certain will be a long road with ever more exciting stops along the way.

Robert Gillmor, P.S.WL.A.
Reading, Berkshire
April 1993

Stilts   1988

Ptarmigan   1989

INTRODUCTION

Some years ago I wanted to produce a book of paintings and sketches based on my own personal observations. It was to be a collection of watercolour impressions of birds gathered from the field. The success of these paintings would, of course, depend on originality and authenticity. I had recently relocated to Wales and it seemed logical that if the studies were to be taken from life, then the Welsh hills and islands would be my study areas.

However, even the most well-planned of journeys does not account for all the discoveries that will be made on the way. I found places of such beauty and richness that no amount of books could do justice to, and I also discovered that I had a lot to learn in the fine art of painting. It may be convenient to say that *Bird Impressions* represents three years' fieldwork, but it would be more accurate to say that it is the result of ten years of learning the craft of field painting. To relate the experience of encounter using the language of paint is both a privilege and a challenge for me. It is a challenge I still at times find difficult, but more importantly it is a challenge I find irresistible.

When compiling the images to be used in the book, there were paintings from earlier years that I wanted to include, as for one reason or another they are valuable to me. The painting of Sandwich Terns was chosen as the inaugural Natural World Art Award winner from works at the Society of Wildlife Artists exhibition in 1987. It was a welcome encouragement at the time as the painting marked a departure in style for me after fumbling with various styles before. The composition was the best in a series of explorations in the medium of watercolour, inspired by the landmark work of Lars Jonsson.

Sandwich Terns – Natural World Art Award   *1987*

Where previously I had drawn shapes and filled in with paint, I was learning how to draw with the brush and use colour to depict light and mood. If the Sandwich Terns were a tribute to Jonsson, then the Eagle Owl could be thought of as a homage to two other great artists, Charles Tunnicliffe and Bruno Liljefors. I had first seen a reproduction of Tunnicliffe's Eagle Owl in *Portrait of a Country Artist,* and another small copy I later pinned on my studio wall. When I was lucky enough to see the original in a private collection it was like seeing an old friend, the image was so familiar to me. It was a large vertical portrait with the bird taking up the whole of the composition and demanding attention. The room it was hanging in was full of other classic Tunnicliffe works, and I remember smiling broadly as I entered. Around the walls were *Curlews in the Rain; Green, Gold and Dun,* and other gems, but it was the presence of *Le Grand Duc* that somehow dominated. Liljefors used Eagle Owls as subjects for many of his paintings, choosing snow, rocks and dense forest as backgrounds. Whether his birds were resting with smouldering eyes or swooping with outstretched talons, the images he presented were always stunning. One painting in particular was a fine composition of a glowing bird set amongst cool rocks at sundown, full of light and rich saturated colour. My painting then was an attempt at fusing both Tunnicliffe and Liljefors birds, bringing together the composition and presence of the former with the colour and drama of the latter.

Eagle Owl

I am often asked why I paint and if there is any message that I am trying to convey through my art, perhaps an indication of the fact that everyone it seems has an opinion and a message these days. Discussions with other artists on the rare occasions of group meetings seem to revolve around art, emotional response and other intangibles. I don't know whether it is a desire to avoid confrontation or a background of a science-based education, but I invariably find myself using a factual and less emotional vocabulary to put my thoughts on wildlife art in context.

Perhaps wildlife painting has a contribution to make in the raising of awareness of conservation issues but, as with many emotive subjects, perhaps other art forms are less limited and better equipped to inform more explicitly. Film and photography are much more accessible media and can unquestionably influence larger numbers of people. There is an undeniable element of realism unique to the camera, and if an important message is to be relayed, then I feel that film is a more provocative and effective medium. Certainly, Frans Lanting's photographs of Madagascan hills denuded of rain forest have impassioned me more than most wildlife paintings.

I would never suggest that the work presented here in *Bird Impressions* can throw any light upon current environmental issues facing us, but I do see the paintings as celebrations of the precious wildlife I have had the luck to encounter, and perhaps a reminder of the beauty which may be lost to future generations.

This sentiment is, of course, not unique. In 1990 a small group from the Netherlands, comprising painters and an art promoter, invited wildlife artists from around the world to meet on the Dutch island of Schiermonnikoog. The impulse to portray the wonder of natural history, common to all painters there, was enough to ensure a successful meeting. More importantly, ideas were exchanged and developed, and the concept of an Artists for Nature Foundation born. Wildlife painters share an enthusiasm which, if focused collectively, could perhaps draw attention to the natural glory that we all know must be preserved.

So in May 1992 at the Bierbrza Valley, Poland, the first meeting of the Artists for Nature Foundation was held. The story is now well documented and illustrated in a beautiful book, supported by an exhibition that is to tour many countries. Inclusions here may seem inappropriate, but both Schiermonnikoog and Biebrza meetings were very happy occasions for me, and if *Bird Impressions* was truly to reflect the fieldwork and paintings of the last three years, then images of Shrikes, Cranes and Storks belong.

Red-backed Shrike – Schiermonnikoog

ACKNOWLEDGEMENTS

Painting may be thought of as a singular pursuit, but the efforts and ideas for the production of a book is certainly collective.

In preparing work for *Bird Impressions,* I have stayed in some wonderful places and at the expense of some special people. My sincere thanks are due to: Paul, Chris and Jaye Rogers at Shorelands; Steve and Anne Sutcliffe, on Skomer; and Kim Atkinson and Gwydion Morley on Bardsey. My thanks also to all my friends at the RSPB Wales office, especially Graham Williams, Alistair Moralee, Jon Porter and Arfon Hughes for making possible my stay on The Skerries. A big thank you also to Ysbrand and Etha Brouwers, Robin D'Arcy Shillcock and all at the Artists for Nature Foundation.

For the production of the book, I would like to record my gratitude to all collectors who generously gave permission to photograph paintings, Vicky Davies for helping with the typing, photographer Colin Jones, designer Glyn Griffin, and Alastair Simpson at Swan Hill Press for showing such faith in the project.

My special thanks to Robert Gillmor. Over many years his wise words, helpful comments and insight have meant so much, and I am truly grateful and privileged that he has contributed the Foreword.

My love and thanks to my family, especially mum and dad, for their unending supply of care and support and, finally, my biggest thanks and love to my wife, Gwynneth, without whom this book would not be possible.

Darren Rees, Newtown, February 1993

Cranes – Biebrza

Storks – Waniewo

Shorelands in January

On the Cefni estuary on Anglesey, overlooking the mud and waders, there is a very special house called *Shorelands*. The artist Charles Tunnicliffe chose to live here, and all around are the birds and scenes made so familiar by his beautiful paintings. Some things have changed since Tunnicliffe worked here, most obviously the huge conifer plantation on the opposite side of the estuary. Newborough Warren is no longer the system of maritime dunes where Montague Harriers and Merlins nested, but now one long strip of regimented pines. Malltraeth village is perhaps busier and the Cefni river has changed its course a little, but the magic that attracted Tunnicliffe here remains in abundance. Cob Pool is still crammed full of ducks, the estuary still brimming with waders, and the view of the Snowdonia range still magnificent.

Shorelands is now the home of Paul, Christine and Jaye Rogers, who use the house as a centre for wildlife holidays. In the spring of 1989 I knocked on their door, as I had been told that they were looking for someone to lead their planned bird-painting courses. As luck would have it, Paul suffers from the same affliction as many bird-watchers – myself included – that of buying too many bird books. Just two weeks prior, he had taken delivery of a book that I had illustrated – I could not have primed him better myself. He loved both book and illustrations, and the course was mine. Several courses and numerous visits later Paul, Chris and Jaye are firm friends and the bird-painting course a regular event in the *Shorelands* year.

Dawn

Wigeon

It is early morning and the panorama
from Tunnicliffe's studio takes on
magical proportions. The mountains of
Snowdonia and the Lleyn Peninsula are
clearly defined, and the pink sun is lifting
through the grey. A line of wader
silhouettes sit on the mud near the
water's edge. Their shape says Lapwing.
The sun's reflection illuminates a small
patch in the channel between the mud
and the rocks, and the water glistens.
Wigeon swim across the light, and their
wake shoots electric blue.

Cob Pool

In front of me is the frozen Cob Pool, with an assortment of teal, pintail and mallard. Dunlin twist across the groups of resting wildfowl and shelducks fly overhead. The drakes utter their contact call and remind me of whirring skipping-ropes in a school playground. Coots arrive on the ice like children on their first outing at the skating rink; slipping and sliding with exuberance and not worrying too much about people laughing at them.

The Pintails are irresistible and my pencil fumbles for their shape. The drakes must surely be the most elegant of wildfowl. Other species may be brighter and more colourful but the graceful proportions and bold markings of the group of males in front of me makes me forget the cold. The fluent forms of the sleeping birds are distorted by the ice, as no part of their volumes is submerged. The light falls across the musculature of the folded neck and breast, and I play with an arrangement of two birds, placing the light of one against the shade of the other. Their Bourneville heads resonate in the late afternoon sun.

Pintail pair – Cob Pool

Teal Threesome

It has been another clear, crisp winter's day and I have spent both morning and afternoon sitting and overlooking the ducks and waders of Cob Pool. During the last couple of hours, singles and small groups of birds have been taking-off and flying over me to the estuary beyond. With fewer and fewer models to draw, I switch my attention from the departing Pintails to a small trio of sleeping Teal. Their reflections in the still water are mirror images and I do not alter anything from the perfect composition before me.

I am aware of the steady trickle of all the birds from the pool, save the three Teal. Finally, even they raise their heads and realise it is time to go. I lift my eyes from the telescope, drop my brushes and stand to stretch my stiff legs.

I turn to look behind to the estuary. The mud is sparkling with a thousand foraging birds. The sun that has been colouring the Teal is now tinting the sky. The headland of Bodorgan divides the pink from the shimmering tidal flats, and I have to pick my brushes up again.

Teal Collection

At the far end of Cob Pool the Teal are gathered. Groups of both sexes are resting in the water and on the edge of the reeds and mud. Sitting still on the exposed bank the wind soon chills my fingers. The pencil feels clumsy in my gloved hand and my sketches are bigger than usual. Pushing the graphite around the pad, using the full width for the darker tones, the birds' shapes are soon described. Most of them are asleep and the back of the heads on the drakes have a hammerhead profile recalling Mandarins. Through the telescope the collection reminds me of a decorative Tunnicliffe composition. It's as if I am watching the same birds.

Signs of Spring

Shorelands in early spring has a wide variety of visitors. Wader numbers are swollen with birds moving through, adding to the resident and winter flocks. From my bed, through the night, I hear whinnying Whimbrel joining the chorus of Curlews. The Oystercatchers and Redshank remain the noisiest though, their shrieks and cries sounding at times so desperate.

The day-time tide pushes up the channel and brings birds nearer and nearer the house. Curiously the Whimbrel seem less timid and there are some birds walking beneath the studio window. One individual sits amongst the rough grass so close that the head fills the frame through my telescope. Perhaps the newcomers have seen no reason to be afraid yet, or perhaps they are just more inquisitive – who knows? The Redshank keep a more respectful distance and pick through the green rocks across the channel. Perhaps they know that Paul will soon be walking the dog.

Shelduck and Heron

The Shelducks on Cob Pool are shining. To draw their shape and faintly colour the water would fail to show their brilliance. The blue-grey of the water needs to be pitched at such a strength as to push the birds out and I test for the tonal value in my small sketchbook.
A Heron flies by low along the creek that feeds the pool. It barks as it sees me and veers violently away. It is more alarmed than I, having failed to notice me any sooner, tucked as I am below the skyline. It is surprising how often birds will not see an observer who has sat still long enough. It flies to the far end of the pool, lands and starts stalking. The landscape is one of horizontal bands with the Heron's elongated shape providing the ideal compositional foil.

Snowdonia and the Cambrian Range

The mountains of North and Central Wales offer some of the most dramatic scenery in Britain, and fittingly Snowdonia was one of the first areas given National Park status in 1951. It is the land of soaring Buzzards, tumbling Ravens and diving Peregrines. Here the landscape is magnificent and dominant, and the birds are small specks sailing across muscular skylines.

The resident breeders turn their thoughts to pairing early in the year and it is not unusual to see displaying raptors as early as February. The escarpment at Dylife is a perfect place to watch birds of prey soaring, plummeting and patrolling the skies. Buzzards gain lift on the updraught that plays along the ridge. They hang suspended on the air current, head fixed, with just minor adjustments here and there to the tail and wing trim. Kites, too, hunt over the adjacent expanse of moor, and glide overhead. Above the rock face, Ravens run through their acrobatic routines and I find it difficult to believe that they are not enjoying the show. From my vantage point while I painted this landscape I saw all those birds, some near, some distant. With the addition of Peregrines, Kestrel and displaying Sparrowhawk, it was a good day's raptor viewing as well as a good day's painting.

Black Grouse

Other spring rites are being enacted in the mountains. The conifer plantations are quiet places, save for a few Chaffinches and Meadow Pipits, but in the early morning mists cooing and bubbling noises drift from some of the damp clearings and forest edges. Blackcocks gather at traditional lek sites to joust and posture amongst the hummocks and cotton grass. Glossy males will perform their curious display of bravado, and all for the benefit of the ladies.

Watching grouse lek means getting up early. It is desirable to be in place before the action starts, and if this means crawling through wet grass and fumbling with fasteners on hides in darkness, then so be it. When there are two artists to be squeezed into a tiny canvas construction then comfort gets squeezed out. Discomfort and the pain of a 3.00 a.m. alarm call are forgotten though when the players take centre stage.

Like phantoms they appear. Before the light is strong enough to discern any shape, I can make out vague dark objects moving through the tussocks. Then, white flashes from what I know are the undertail coverts catch my eye, and I start to make sense of the forms. There seems to be three males strutting and sparring and fanning their curved tails. Then the cooing noises intensify as more birds arrive. The bubbling is interspersed with harsher, more explosive, scolding calls and the manoeuvring seems more purposeful. I can now count six cocks

displaying as the light starts to ease over the Berwyn ridge. Soon the full splendour of the birds is revealed as the dawn rays touch them. The black is coated glossy blue, and the red feathers on the head glow like beacons. Flexing their lyres and parading like stars, they prove irresistible and excited females fly in.

We watch enthralled for two hours before the sun finally floods the theatre and the performance peters out. A Hen Harrier beats buoyantly across the heather and grass before us and I realise that the day is just beginning. It is 6.30 a.m.

416/5 Abernbe

River Birds

Mid-Wales is blessed with more than its share of crystal-clear small rivers and streams. These are fed by swift-running brooks that tumble from the surrounding hills and moors. The water, is for the most part, free from the excessive pollutants that blight many lowland courses, and supports healthy populations of freshwater invertebrates. In turn, these are ideal territories for Dippers, and many nest in the area. Dippers then, like Kingfishers and Grey Wagtails, are useful indicators to chart the fortunes of healthy or sick rivers. Fluctuations in the levels of water-borne toxins will correlate to fluctuations in their numbers. As with other large animals, birds are so placed in the food chain that their successes and failures have far-reaching ramifications. Breeding Goosanders and Hen Harriers are positive signs of thriving river and moorland communities, and should be welcomed and not persecuted.

The Mule river is typical of the region. It runs off the border hills and winds its way to the Severn, joining at Abermule. Along its short length several Dipper pairs breed. At the Dingle the valley is at its narrowest and most shaded, and here the overhanging foliage colours the water brown and green. The painting opposite was done *in situ*, and was an attempt to depict the movement, current and colour.

Dapper Dippers

Dippers are such fun to watch, constantly bobbing and busying themselves, and never standing still. Every little river should have one. They fly upstream and downstream on blurred wings, their rasping call giving me notice of their comings and goings. They stand on the wet rocks amid white water and are not nearly as obvious as their bold markings would at first suggest. Their plumage is simple, but smart. The white bib is always neatly cut, and I have never seen a badly-tailored adult.

Ring Ouzel

Wheatear

Blossom

From my studio window I can overlook the hedgerow at the bottom of the garden. It is a tangled mixture of dog rose, hawthorn and blooming blackthorn. Birds have always found refuge amongst the mesh, a place safe from prowling cats and hunting Sparrowhawks. Throughout the winter months I have been entertained by Bullfinches, Nuthatches and Greenfinches, to name but a few, but as the spring advances they seem to keep closer to their breeding areas nearer the river. I am more likely to see Robins, Wrens, Blackbirds and Tree Sparrows. Before April has ended, many migrants have arrived and are looking for territories in the adjacent hills and valleys. Redstarts and Whinchats have joined their eager cousins the Wheatears, and are adding their own colours to the resident bird life. Whinchats are attracted to more open areas than Redstarts and the mosaic of gorse and bracken that covers the hills of much of Mid-Wales is an ideal habitat.

Spring in the Valley

Down-river from Newtown, the Severn valley steadily widens before opening out at its confluence with the Vyrnwy. Three miles from Welshpool, at The Gaer, the river snakes across the flood plain in a succession of leisurely meanders. There are scars of former riverbanks and ox-bow lakes as evidence to its ever-changing course. The stretches of shingle and green meadows are seasonal homes to a variety of birds, including Little Ringed Plovers, Oystercatchers, Yellow Wagtails and Lapwings. Dug into the eroded banks there are Sand Martin colonies, and the air is thick with their twittering.

The Wagtails are difficult to overlook. Their primrose-yellow dazzles the eye. I am sitting painting the Black-headed Gulls that rest obligingly on an island of pebbles, and a Yellow Wagtail distracts me. He crouches in the grass with his head thrown back, flirting his colour and charm.

The Gaer 13·4·89

Darren Rees

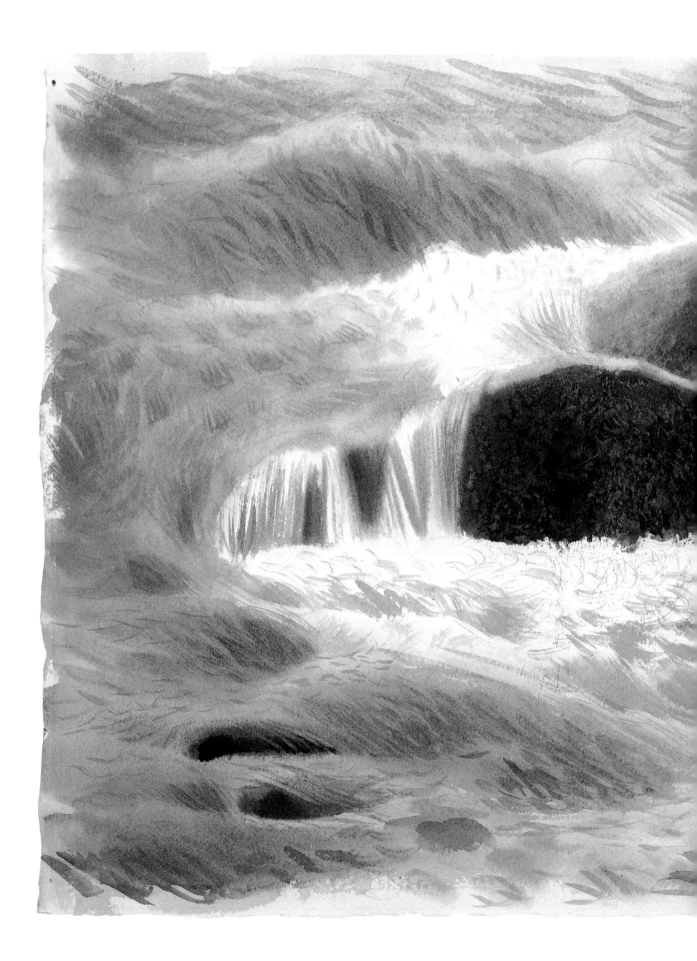

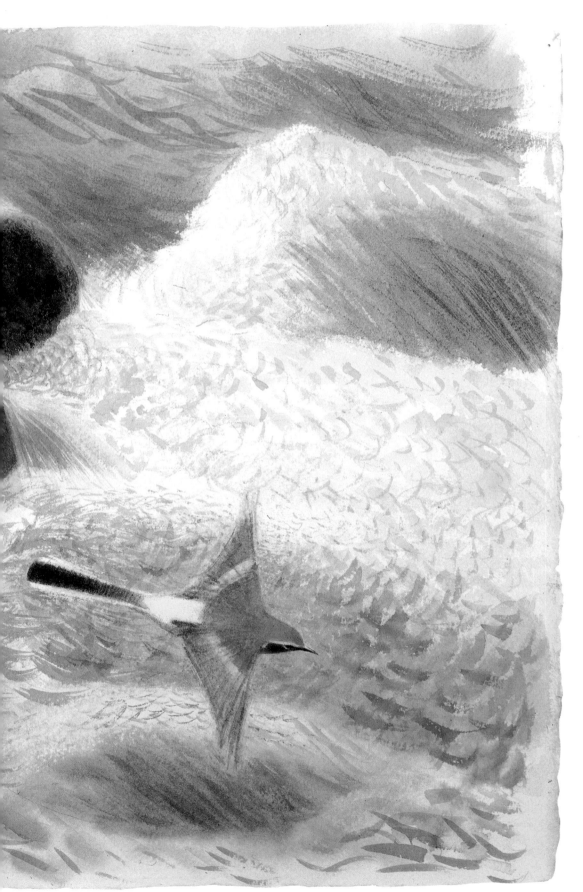

Yellow Streaks

Grey Wagtails are not only grey, but the most vivid of yellows. They bound along river courses in a characteristic undulating flight, their long tail whipping behind. The flash of canary-yellow and explosive *tsee-tit* is diagnostic. Mochdre Brook is just a few hundred yards from the house and is as good a place as any to watch Grey Wagtails.

Most paintings will have a focal point or points, which leave the whole image in equilibrium. In this composition I wanted to express motion and sought a position for the bird that would perhaps leave the picture less balanced and therefore unrestrained. In addition, I wanted to ensure that the bird was flying. It is sometimes difficult to establish wing shape in birds that are small and have quick wing beats. In this instance, I thought that freezing the profile of the flight feathers would be undesirable and stop the action. The painting is an attempt to retain the movement of both bird and water.

Song Thrush

The blackthorn is fading before the hawthorn blooms and the hedgerow takes on a ragged look. A sprinkling of optimistic green pushes through the knotted twigs, and below, petals lie strewn like confetti. A Dunnock creeps along the base of the hedge and wing flaps at his bride.

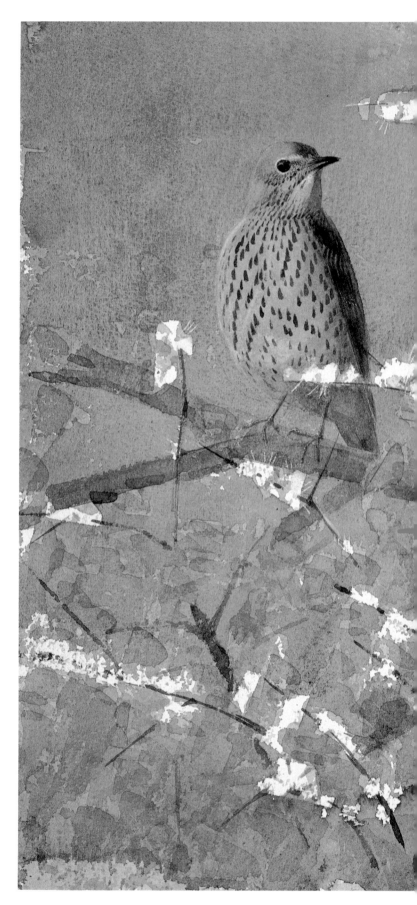

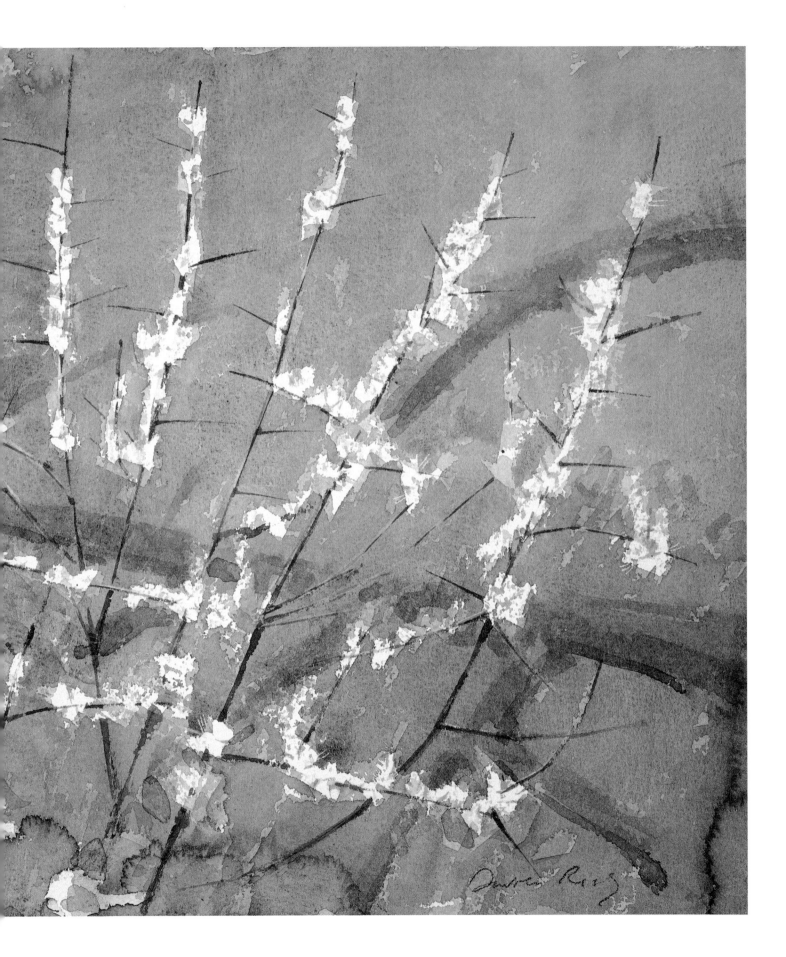

Guillemot – Still Life

South Stack – Anglesey

Summer Islands

Away from the hills and valleys, the breeding season is beginning for seabirds in their thousands. Birds that have spent the winter far out in the Atlantic are now arriving at the cliffs and islands along our western coast. From South Stack on Anglesey to the islands of Pembrokeshire, the scenes are of a teeming bird-life throughout the summer months. Seabird colonies are the most stimulating places to watch nature at its glorious and hectic best. The rugged rock faces are stuffed with Auks and Gulls, courting and fighting, feeding and dying. Cities of birds spew air that is thick with croaks, cries, grunts and the aroma of a million droppings. Any visit to a seabird colony is a memorable one with sights, sounds and smells which work the senses overtime. My first seabird island was Skomer, and I shall never forget that day in May when, like an excited child in a toy shop, I did not know where to look or what to listen to first.

Razorbill – Bull Hole

Skomer

To the west of Pembrokeshire lie the islands of Skomer, Skokholm, Ramsey and Grassholm. Of these, probably the richest for number and variety of birds, and certainly the most accessible, is Skomer. Just two miles of boiling Jack Sound separates it from the mainland, and on most days in the summer the *Dale Princess* is able to ferry visitors the short journey across the straits.

Skomer is a volcanic tableland of 720 acres, rising some 50 to 150 feet above Saint Brides Bay. Between North and South Haven, a narrow isthmus of softer sedimentary rock holds The Neck to the main part of the island. The cliff-tops and interior of the island are covered with thin, sandy soil which has proved easy for birds and rabbits to excavate. The surface is now a fragile honeycomb of burrows that house Puffins, Shearwaters and rabbits. The vegetation that binds the brittle earth is a colourful mixture of heather, bracken, bluebells and red campion, with thrift and sea campion clothing the seaward slopes. The gentle undulations of the inner isle are broken by rocky sills that run sporadically east-west across Skomer's length.

There are only a handful of buildings on the island and there are no permanent inhabitants. At North Haven, above the landing jetty, is the Warden's house, which also doubles as accommodation for research workers. In the centre of the island is an old farmhouse and adjacent buildings. The island has not been worked since 1950 and most of the buildings are shells of their former selves. Some, though, have been renovated and serve as lodgings for volunteer staff and overnight stayers.

The island has been awarded National Nature Reserve status in recognition of its importance as a sea-bird breeding station. Each spring it holds some 160,000 pairs of Manx Shearwaters, which represents a third of the world's population. Similarly, there are significant numbers of Lesser Black-backed gulls, Kittiwakes, Razorbills, Guillemots and Puffins. There are also Storm Petrel, Fulmar, Shag, Raven, Chough, Peregrine, Curlew, Short-eared Owl, Little Owl and others, and it is not an exaggeration to refer to Skomer as a bird paradise.

The Wick

The Wick is an awesome sight. It is a
sheer vertical wall that rises two hundred
feet from the waves. Across its face are
the scars and fractures of countless years
of weathering, but ancient as it is there is
much life here. Clinging to every nook
and crevice and flying in and out are
thousands of birds. The eyes are
bewildered by the numbers, and the ears
are prickled by a cacophony of braying,
cackling and *kiffi-week* cries.

The bird society is layered here. A
necklace of white ledges rings the lower
strata with Guillemots sitting sometimes
five deep along the length. Above are the
Razorbills, tucked away much less
densely and in more sheltered holes.
Interspersed between the two Auk
species are Kittiwakes. They have built
nests that somehow cling to the upright
plane and spot the surface.

Higher still is a long horizontal fissure
that houses several pairs of Fulmars. They
peer out from the crack with their gentle
faces, having the best of views of all from
Wick tenement.

Wick Valley is to the left of the chasm
that the Wick overlooks. Its more gentle
slopes are covered with bluebells and is a
regular feeding spot for Choughs. The
sight of these red-billed Crows foraging
amongst the blue is as memorable a sight
as the Wick itself.

Guillemots

Castle Bay is a small cove on the southeast of Skomer. There is a wooden hide here that peers into the crowded Auk ledges and is the perfect place to watch Guillemots. Well, almost perfect. I am wedged into a small cubicle with drawing boards, paint boxes, telescope and tripod and I reckon that even the Guillemots have more space on their cramped ledges. Then again, I cannot complain; not having bickering neighbours pecking my head and shrieking at me to budge up. Through the narrow window I can watch the everyday happenings of a whole row of chocolate-coloured Guillemots. As I drop the wooden slat I am greeted by their gutteral cries and the sound of pounding waves. Flakes of surf float by on the updraught that fans the scent of guano. I unpack my materials and make myself as comfortable as possible. There are animated disputes over precious square inches of the ledge. The pointed bills which give the Guillemots

such a sleek profile are now wielded as weapons, and all around are fencing necks and heads. One bird flies into a rude reception party and is jostled by the esconced birds, and left no alternative but to take off again. Those that are not arguing are resting and are arched into perfect forms. A strong sun is high behind me and casts perpendicular shadows on the rounded models. I spend most of the day drawing and painting these sleeping beauties.

Other shapes also catch my eye. Some birds are on nests and are crouched with wings lowered, giving the unhatched eggs shelter from the chill sea breeze. A singleton is pressed up to a vertical plane of rock and its body assumes a right angle. Another fight breaks out further along the ledge and two birds tumble off locked in combat. The sleeping birds do not flinch. The scene is both chaotic and tranquil. There is conflict and there is peace.

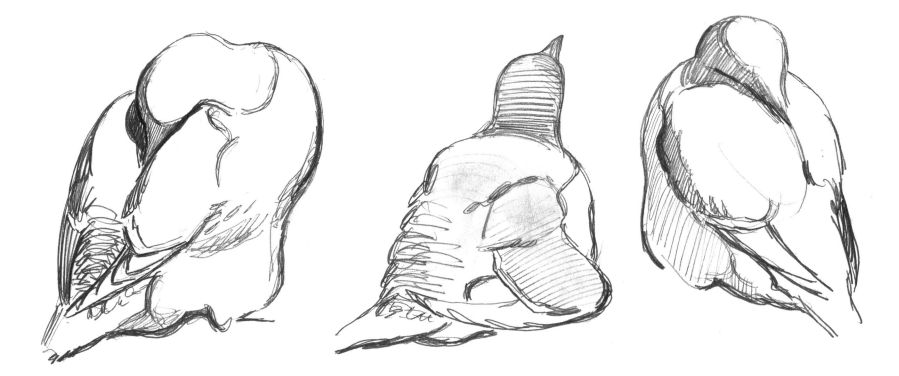

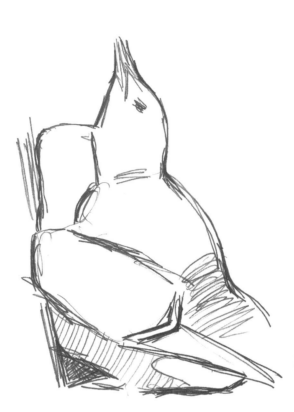

Guillemot Composition

For three consecutive days I sat in the tiny hide at Castle Bay, engrossed with the beauty of Guillemots. The painting opposite is a studio piece using the sketches and coloured fieldwork gathered here.

Guillemots on Skomer – Swarovski Young
European Bird Artist Award   *1991*

Puffins

If there were a survey of people's favourite birds then Puffins would surely figure prominently. They are such comical and engaging characters. Watching them march to and fro like clockwork toys I cannot help but smile and think that Mother Nature has a sense of humour.

At the Wick in the evenings, the Puffins gather.

They arrive on whirring wings, their bright orange undercarriage dropped for the landing in front of me. The first arrivals scurry into the nesting holes down the slope, then others land and walk more tentatively to the burrows that are closer. Some of the painted faces pause and give me an anxious stare before resuming their awkward steps towards me. One by one they pace through the campion, each bird seemingly a little more daring than the previous. I gingerly unpack my art materials and start to work, carefully trying not to make any sudden motions. As the light lowers and the evening wears on the whole group seems oblivious to me. They have accepted the stranger amongst them and around me are Puffins so close that my telescope and binoculars are redundant. The resting birds are unconcerned by the rattling of my paint tin as I mix the pigments. The clowns are quiet.

Skomer Head

It is a clear evening in June, and after yet another supper of packet soup I tread the path between the farmhouse and the west of the island. The Curlew parent is standing sentinel and is as anxious as ever as I pass by. Its mantle and scapular feathers are raised with agitation, and the bird cuts an angular silhouette. It gives a series of alarm cries which I presume is Curlewspeak for "here comes trouble". The chicks are somewhere in the bluebells and bracken, so I only make a quick note and then move on to avoid the din. As I near the clifftop an Oystercatcher hurls more abuse from the rocks which hides its nest scrape. It must be a trying time raising a family on Skomer.

I approach Skomer Head which forms the south-west corner of the island. Before me, the pink thrift trembles in the stiff breeze that is ever-present here. Looking south-east, the rugged southern cliffs of Skomer tumble seawards. The successive headlands of Tom's House, The Wick and The Mewstone draw the eye back to the distant Pembrokeshire mainland. The views arrest me.

Offshore to the west, thousands of Shearwaters are gathering, waiting for darkness. It is past nine o'clock and the falling sun is colouring the water with a shimmering array of pinks and yellows. The blue and purple shadows of the waves add texture, and across the scene an endless train of Shearwaters passes. They traverse effortlessly with long glides interspersed with a few shallow beats of their stiff wings. The helpless birds I had watched just a couple of nights earlier on the ground are now doing what they do best.

Shearwaters off Skomer Head – End of Day

The Skerries

The Skerries lie due north of Holyhead, eight miles out to sea. A tiny outcrop of rugged islets, they number only 42 acres and are dominated by the red and white bulk of a Trinity House light. The low-lying rocks are unsuitable for some bird species like Guillemots and Razorbills, but the other bird-life is that typical of many west coast islands with Shags, Oystercatchers, Herring and Lesser Black-backed Gulls, Kittiwakes and a small group of Puffins. The main attraction though is the large Arctic Tern colony that covers the centre of the island, and some 300 pairs nest amongst the rocks and sea-spurrey that surround the lighthouse. This number represents an important breeding group nationally and each summer wardens from the Royal Society for the Protection of Birds are based on the Skerries to monitor the term's successes and failures. For an all-too-short time one summer I was allowed to take my paints and sketch pads and witness the daily happenings on this tiny paradise in the Irish Sea.

My passage to the Skerries was aboard the weekly supply boat that delivers beer, chocolate biscuits and other essentials to the needy wardens. Jon Porter and Arfon Hughes were now the sole inhabitants of these rocks, the lighthouse being fully automated and the keepers long since gone. Both had been forewarned that a painter was coming to stay and the thought had occurred to me that they might be expecting me to give the lighthouse a new coat of *Weathershield*! The boat eased into the sheltered natural harbour and the seals basking on the rocks gave us a cursory glance before resuming their banana-like poses. Jon and Arfon were at the landing steps and the huge red and white light towered behind them. Lighthouses are such functional buildings. From afar they are immaculate, shining fortresses, but on closer inspection they are surrounded by pipes, portacabins and the paraphernalia of self-sufficiency. This, then, was to be my temporary home.

Introductions dispensed with at the landing site, we quickly took the supplies and my luggage to the shelter of the lighthouse. Having established that I was not there to maintain the waterproof properties of the lighthouse, we were soon discussing Terns, chicks, Peregrine predation and exactly how many beers I had brought.

Bundles of Fluff

Nature came up with a cunning design for Tern chicks with the blotches on a brown upperside and the pale belly making for a cryptic plumage. In most light conditions, when a simple shadow might reveal the form of a chick, the tone of the whitish belly is similar to that of the rest of the body and makes the young bird difficult to detect. In addition, the markings and soft feathering break up the outline and it is easy to loose the chick amongst the rocks and vegetation, particularly so when mother screams out, 'Make like a stone!' With the aid of a telescope though, I can sit at a distance from the colony and watch the bundles of fluff without upsetting their parents. Sketching them, I'm looking for features other than colour and blotches, to help me make sense of their form. Only when a chick tries a flew flaps of their stubby wings can I make the merest semblance of the fore-limbs. They scurry around on tiny red feet begging for food from the adult birds, or collapse exhausted on full stomachs saving their energy for the next round of frantic activity.

Most often the parent Tern brings tiny sandeels for the chicks, but on one occasion the adult brought what I took to be a sprat. It was as long as the fledgling yet, undaunted, the young bird opened wide and attempted to consume the fish. I watched in amazement as the chick sat upright, the posture dictated by the stiffness of the fish, with a third of the sprat poking out of the gaping beak. I presumed that the chick would either choke or try to eject the fish, or do both, but it just sat there! For five minutes I watched and tried to imagine what it was like to swallow a whole pig, then the chick gulped a few more millimetres down. Incredibly, it seemed the digestive system was already breaking down the head of the fish before the tail was inside. Every few minutes a few more gulps and another couple of millimetres disappeared. Soon only the tail fin was left, and five minutes later even that had vanished. The chick had doubled its weight in ten minutes and remained there, bolt upright, gasping for air. Within half an hour the bird had managed to move to a more comfortable position but I didn't see it eat any more that day.

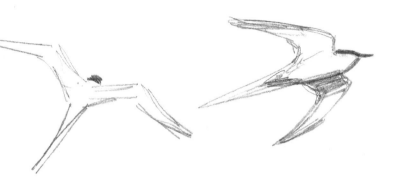

Tern Fishing

Between the rocks and outlying islets the tidal races swell. Flat bands of swirling water flow between surging seas. The water dynamics seem to stir the small fry close to the surface and these are the favourite fishing sites for the Terns. The endless cycle of parent birds hunting and feeding unfolds before me. Like white sprites they hover over the grey seas then dive to pierce the shoals of fish. They return after each sortie to the gapes of their hungry chicks. The fish is deposited then they are off again on another circuit. Birds going out weave past birds coming in. There is a rhythm and an order amongst the chaos. When painting, I am always looking for these patterns and rhythms. The methods I employ with watercolours demand this. To express a complex rhythm using a few brushstrokes makes one impose a more simple order. In particular with this painting the task was to take the continuum of water, with its myriad patterns and patterns within patterns, and break it down to a body with fewer separate elements. I've attempted to let the brush flow with the dynamics of the water. Sharp, straight strokes here, crisp crescent curves there. The positioning of the birds, too, has been chosen to best pace the painting. The left-hand figures hover, the middle figures fly directly and the right-hand figure circles back to the viewer to complete the cycle.

Sleeping Seals

The southern-most finger of land encloses a large shallow and sheltered lagoon which is the only safe place for boats to land on the Skerries. The calm water also attracts Grey Seals keen to take an afternoon nap. Their huge bodies, so graceful in the water, are now cumbersome on the rocks. Some haul themselves from the sea with jerking efforts that ripple their blubber. Other seals are balancing on submerged rocks, and as the tide level drops they seem to defy gravity with their considerable curved bulks resting on the water. I watch them scratch and stretch, but for the most part they just doze. The sun smacks their sleeping faces and I imagine how good it is to be a seal. They seem untroubled by Third World debt and rain forest depletion, but perhaps they may have some choice words on pollution levels in the Irish Sea.

I spend the afternoon and evening with the lounging seals before it starts to drizzle. I would normally avoid painting in a shower, but on this occasion the effect of rain on watercolours seems desirable. The droplets pepper the surface of the paint and curiously mimic the blotches on the seal's coat. Working from life has its happy accidents.

Kittiwake – Skerries

To the Landing Steps

The one path leading from the lighthouse to the landing steps runs through part of the Tern colony. Walking along the track can be a perilous business and a government health warning might seem appropriate. Terns are nervous at the best of times and they do not tolerate humans near their chicks. Trespassers trigger an eruption of screaming birds and are dive-bombed and harried relentlessly. As the Terns swoop they emit an unnerving clicking noise, the frequency increasing the nearer they get to your head. They regularly make contact and their sharp beaks can easily draw blood. Often as not, though, they just leave their white, slimy calling card. A thought occurred to me of how best to cope with these aerial bombardments. I could run around using a canvas as a cover and collect the guano splatters. After one week I should have a veritable Jackson Pollock-ful of droppings. Such are the idle thoughts of someone marooned mid-Irish Sea.

Once at the steps, the fuss soon dies down and the scene is peaceful. It has become a favourite place for me to paint in the afternoons. Not only are the seals relaxing close by, but the Kittiwakes are gathered on the rocks opposite. Also an Oystercatcher has raised two chicks on the rocks to the right of the landing stage and I am spoilt for choice of subjects.

Peregrines

The success story of the rise in numbers of Peregrines after the crash in their population in the 1950s is well documented and familiar to most people. The remote areas of the North and West were their last refuges during their years of decline, but they are now breeding in other haunts throughout Britain. Their range has expanded from their mountain and coastal stronghold to nests at cliff faces, quarries and even urban sites. For the moment their immediate future seems secure. The Peregrines I have watched most closely are a pair that have nested for the last three seasons in a quarry in Montgomeryshire.

The chicks shown here were sketched at different stages in their development. The incubating adult was drawn from a pair nesting on Anglesey.

It is important to note that Peregrines are listed as Schedule 1 birds under the Wildlife and Countryside Act 1981, and it is an offence to disturb them at the nest. Both sites represented here were observed through high magnification optical equipment.

Sleeping Sentinel

The eyrie is opposite me at some distance, though through my telescope I can see the chicks clearly. A small hawthorn bush gives some shade and cover and, littered though the nest is with feathers, bones and droppings, the site is not obvious. The parent birds are absent but I know they both cannot be far. Usually as one hunts the other stands sentinel.

I pick up my binoculars and search the quarry. A strong sun moulds hollow shadows from the sombre rock face and I pan through the light and shade. The male is not difficult to find. The tell-tale droppings lead me to his favourite perches and I spot his white face against the grey. He is on guard duty while the female is searching for food. He has chosen a platform that juts out from the quarry face. He is presented on some purpose-made plinth sculpted from the rock and I watch him as he sits. I notice moments of laxness as he dozes with first one eye closed and then both. Perhaps like Ted Hughes' *Hawk Roosting* he rehearses perfect kills in his sleep, but rehearse suggests some element of chance and I only see perfection.

Bird Rock

The Dysynni valley in Snowdonia falls from Cader Idris south and west to Merionnydd coast. In the thirteenth century a barrier was constructed at the mouth of the estuary and the valley floor silted up. The land was then drained and reclaimed for simple farming purposes. Now the valley profile is steep-sided with a broad, flat bottom. In the middle of the valley, standing proud and tall, is Bird Rock. Traditionally this has been a nesting site for Cormorants as it was once a sea cliff. Now it is six miles from salt water, but the Cormorants have remained faithful and fly up and down the valley to nest. In addition it is an inland site for breeding Choughs, and both Peregrine and Raven can frequently be seen on the rockface.

Wild Moor

The high tops are lonely places, empty of people but nonetheless full of colour and texture. These are lands fashioned by the elements. Racing clouds throw racing shadows over the quivering heather and molinia grass. Those trees that dare grow here cower in the lee of rocks or stand exposed, stunted and teased into shape by the wind.

The birdlife here would be described as specialist rather than rich. Three birds of prey have adjusted to these bleak terrains – the Merlin, the Hen Harrier and the Short-eared Owl. Merlins have adapted to feeding on aerial prey such as Meadow Pipits and Skylarks and their hunting technique has attuned accordingly. Their flight is fast and direct and frankly difficult to watch and draw. Both Hen Harrier and Short-eared Owl though have slower flights, relying on stealth rather than speed to catch most of their prey on the ground. They float unhurried over the moors quartering their territories with buoyant wing beats, to suddenly twist and drop in the rough grass. I could watch them all day, and indeed on many occasions I have.

Summer's End

The summer colours seem tired and past their sell-by date. The expanses of green could do with a sweep and fungi are pushing up through the litter – it is a time for wild mushroom soup. The birdlife is showing promises of things to come as I notice brilliant young Leaf Warblers moving along the hedgerow in the garden. It is a time though to look at the constants and standards of common birds before enjoying the more unusual. Pheasant populations are at a peak before the guns are set mercilessly on them. However you view their introduction and nurturing they are now very much part of the British landscape, and who could deny the cock pheasant his ornateness?

Pheasant and Fungi

Herring Gull

Bardsey

Bardsey lies off the south-west tip of the Lleyn Peninsula in North Wales. From the cliffs above Aberdaron its tapered form looks like some giant jockey cap, but this view is misleading. Most of the island is hidden from view by Mynydd Enlli, optimistically termed the mountain, which rises to a modest 167 metres. Its bracken and gorse-covered slopes take up nearly half the island and to the east these plunge to the sea in a series of dramatic cliffs. To the south and west the descent is more gentle and the land spreads out over small fields and damp withys, before ending abruptly with rugged low-lying rocks.

The south of the island is pinched at the Narrows by two opposing shallow coves; Solfach on the wild, west side and Henllwyn on the sheltered east.

There are a dozen or so buildings either side of the rough track that runs along the north-south axis of the island. On the southern plateau, and at one end of the track, is the lighthouse, and at the north and other end are the ruins of a thirteenth century Augustinian abbey. Sprinkled inbetween are a collection of sturdy dwellings including the farmhouse, estate house, small cottages and the observatory.

Like many of the islands off our western coast, Bardsey is a seabird haven. It was one of the first bird observatories to be

Yellow-browed Warbler

established, in 1953, and more recently, in 1986, it was designated a National Nature Reserve. As well as being an important breeding refuge for many species, each autumn Bardsey attracts a large number of migrants. Birds from the north are funnelled through the peninsula and pause on Bardsey off the southern point. On overcast moonless nights thousands of thrushes can be attracted to the lighthouse beam. Blizzards of birds are illuminated by the sweeping light and the night sky resembles a giant firework display. Many drop exhausted to the ground, some die from hitting the light, and others wander dazed around the lighthouse compound. These are carefully picked up and placed in bags for ringing and weighing. There can be an assortment of species with such falls, from gentle Storm Petrels and dainty Blackcaps to gangly Water Rails. The latter refuse to fold their legs away without a struggle. The morning after a fall of migrants can see the bushes all over the island dripping with birds. Looking through forty years of records of birds on Bardsey the list of species is considerable, with many unusual waifs and strays turning up in the months of September and October. Like the Yellow-browed Warbler I am an autumn migrant to the island, though I hope that I visit a little more frequently.

Wryneck

News travels fast on an island and when it's news of an unusual bird it travels even faster. The impact of the telecommunications revolution is far reaching indeed, but no paging device can match Bardsey's own rapid information relay system. When a rarity is found on the island a bright coloured marker buoy is hoisted on the observatory wall and this can be seen immediately from all points. Simple but effective.

This morning the signal had been raised and I had been told that there was a Wryneck in the lane leading from the Withys to Cristin. I marched across the fields to where a handful of birdwatchers were gathered, standing in a rough semi-circle, all with binoculars raised and pointing in the same direction – it was still there!

Only one week earlier I had been lucky enough to be in Majorca when many migrant Wrynecks were passing through. Their Kestrel-like cries were heard in the scrub and bushes, mountains and marshes, and even from the swimming pool. They are notoriously elusive birds and give only tantalising glimpses, rarely staying still long enough to view through a telescope. However, on Bardsey there are few places to hide and this individual sat in the open, in the drizzle, attracting inquisitive looks from the local Stonechats and Meadow Pipits. My pencil moved across the damp pages of my sketchbook and I cursed myself for not bringing soluble graphite. I persevered having presumed that this Wryneck would behave as any other and soon seek cover. Either I was lucky or this bird was an exhibitionist, for the drizzle ended and the Wryneck remained and started to feed.

7·10

Seals at Henllwyn

The Grey Seals shown here were painted at Henllwyn bay where there are always individuals hauled out on the rocks at high tide. The honey-coloured coat on the seal shown above indicates that it is a yearling.

Little Owl

Bardsey enjoys a healthy population of Little Owls with several pairs holding territories each year. There are many suitable outcrops of rock on the mountain and they also inhabit the turf and stone walls that criss-cross the island. Owls have always been favourite subjects of anthropomorphism, and watching them closely it is not difficult to see why. The feathered discs around the eyes and binocular visual arrangement gives the owl an identifiable face. With the Little Owl the irises are pale and the eyes piercing. The facial disc has been modified to a brow over the eye and it can look like the bird is frowning. When alarmed this brow is less pronounced and the eyes seem to show expressions of surprise. Coupled with a hunched or upright posture it is easy to imagine moods of scowling indifference or wide-eyed excitement.

In the late afternoons and evenings they are at their most vocal and their hoarse cries can be heard from most places on the island. This is probably the best time to watch them if only because they are easier to locate. The lower angle of the sun at this time of day creates more interesting light effects such as the rim-lit bird shown here.

Solfach

The bay at Solfach is a shallow sandy cove with low-lying rocky flanks. It has that inviting unkempt look of stranded flotsam and discarded seaweed. At low tide the wrack and kelp carpets the lower beach with a colour tangle of sienna and umber. On Bardsey the sheep delight in nibbling the seaweed – a sight to which I am unaccustomed. A dozen ewes are grazing with their heads down before me. There is a pair of Choughs on the beach too. Both are gleaning tit-bits from the tideline, and are conspicuous with their loud metallic calls and shiny black coats. Turnstones have been feeding along the shore in front of the tide. When they are foraging, and indeed turning stones, their plumage appears as random blocks of colour, but when they fly they reveal more ordered markings. A group flies by, showing alternate views of their underside and topside. First I see the brilliant white bellies and then the striking patterns of the upper parts and wings. The change in the pied arrangement moves through the group in an harmonic wave as they fly across the bay.

A flock of Starlings wheels around over the headland to the left and I instinctively look to the sky for a raptor. Their eyes are sharper than mine and I fail to see the danger as she passes low over the sand and rocks. Hugging the curve of the bay I only spot her when she flies by in front of me. A female Merlin flashes through.

Watching Choughs

Another windy day and I choose the cover of Solfach's hide to sketch from. Before me the seaweed sprawls like a thousand rusting pipes. Many birds are picking through the debris looking for food and I lift my binoculars for a closer look. The seaweed is alive with Starlings and Pipits moving like a plague of mice through the litter. Two Yellow Wagtails weave a lemon trail and a Wheatear bounces along the sand. Some Starlings are hitching a ride on the back of a sheep while others are drying and preening after their morning bath. They shiver and shake so vigorously that I expect their spots to loosen.

The hide at Solfach is not only one of the few sheltered places on the island but it is also one of the best sites to view Choughs. Pairs of birds bound across the bay and land on the beach to forage amongst the weed for invertebrates. I haven't finished unpacking my paints and pencils when a glossy couple land and announce themselves with a loud *kcheeow*. They take one look around, flick their wings and call again, then launch into energetic feeding. Using their bills like shiny red pick axes, they hack at the tangled weed. Their bodies are tilted head-down, tail up, and their under-tail coverts hang open below. The wings become disshevelled in the wind and I struggle to find order in the raggedness of the rear of each bird. There is no strong light and the feathering on the body appears more velvet than gloss. I've watched Chough in varying conditions and nearly always the mantle and head plumage will absorb the light, giving a matt black look with the green sheen appearing only on the wings and tail. I watch the birds for most of the day before the wind whistling through the windows in the hide finally beats me into submission. The thought of a hot tea wins out and I convince myself that I'll be able to paint much better with warmer hands.

Seawatching

The forecast for high winds from the north-west is bad news for anyone wishing to cross Bardsey Sound, but good news for birdwatchers already staying on the island. In such conditions birds passing through the Irish Sea are blown nearer Bardsey and binoculars and telescopes are trained on the sea. The hide at the most northerly tip of the island gives some shelter from the wind and spray, and is where I head for.

Far out there is a steady passage of birds moving south. Through the telescope I scan between the middle distance and horizon. The magnitude of the waves is only realised when I see Gannets disappearing into deep troughs to re-appear many second later. The birds that I can see must represent only a small proportion of the birds I cannot see.

The waves move with a relentless hypnotism broken by pulses of birds. Most numerous are the Auks that stream by on frantic wing-beats. Kittiwakes fly by with less rapid beats and their neat, black wing tips are clearly visible. They look like they have been dipped in ink. A train of dark Scoter passes by in characteristic fashion and steadily the species count increases.

Then the first of the Skuas move menacingly through. I have been expecting them. There is something distinct about their silhouette that leaves no confusion with immature Gulls. They appear much darker, and the wing-beats are deeper and more purposeful. They know where they are going. There are three Arctic Skuas passing at varying distances, only on the nearest bird can I detect the thin tail streamers. The individuals further away show just a tapered appearance.

A much more solid-looking bird with larger white wing patches enters from the right. It is a Great Skua. Compared with the lithe Arctic Skuas the Bonxie seems bulky and ponderous but it shines as it passes.

Wild Waves and Struggling Guillemots

If yesterday's sea was raging then today's is a tempest. From Solfach hide the water looks like a cauldron with the breaking surf whipping the sea white. The howling wind has increased in strength and has shaken the water like a fizzy drink. The speed is now force nine to ten and very few birds are moving by. Some Herring Gulls have battled by on bent wings, but there are a fraction of the numbers of the previous day. The Auks still struggle by on blurred wings, beating furiously so as not to fly backwards in the gale. Only when they pass more closely can I begin to separate the Guillemots from the less frequent Razorbills. The former are more cleanly marked about the face and the bill profile gives a more attenuated shape compared to the blunt Razorbill.

I note their simple outline and begin to tackle painting the mountainous sea. With so much white to depict I chose to exploit the roughness of the paper. Using a drier brush technique the strokes breaks up and leaves white textured area. A heavyweight support also allows me to attack the surface with a blade. As the brush layers are applied to convey the inexorable rhythm of the crashing waves, so too is the scalpel worked to explore the patterns of the surf.

Shags

Shags come in one size but lots of different shapes. Shags, and indeed their cousins the Cormorants, adopt an array of contortions to entertain the eye. Each successive pose presents new arrangements of feather and muscle and new proportions of neck-to-body length. To borrow a phrase from John Busby, they are an endless source of delight for any collector of bird shapes. The individuals here are the lighter-coloured immatures that spent most days resting and preening in the bays of Solfach and Henllwyn.

Winter Birds

The winter landscape may lack the immediate richness of spring and summer scenes, but after watching birds feeding in my garden I am left with no doubt that there is no shortage of colour. The winter months are often the best time to see woodland species, with no foilage to hinder viewing and a paucity of foodstuff forcing many to supplement their intake with the nuts hanging outside my studio window.

For anyone wishing to draw birds, Blue Tits on garden feeders are good places to start. Sitting on bleak estuaries might seem daunting to beginners, but what could be more comfortable than sketching familiar birds through a window from the warmth of indoors. Blue Tits may be restless and can flit and jerk every which way, but patience and effort will usually be rewarded. The process of sitting and looking will not only help to understand the nuances of their simple shape, but also reveal patterns of behaviour that may be easily overlooked. Drawing is the business of learning and two hours spent observing and sketching Blue Tits is far greater education than slavishly mimicing a photograph.

Unexpected Visitors

Shrikes are nice birds.
Unless you're a beetle that is. Their predilection for impaling prey and leaving them wriggling and twitching on thorns does little for their chances in Insects Review's "Bird Personality of the Year" Award. However, I am not an insect. I like Shrikes.

I mention this as many people have asked me what is my favourite bird. It is of course a question with no single answer. Watch any bird closely from humble Tree Sparrows to boldly-marked Shelduck, and I enter their world and fall for their charm. There are some birds however that I am particularly attracted to and of these, the Red-backed Shrike is undoubtedly one. Indeed the whole Shrike family has to be included, they are such perfectly proportioned birds.

One lucky day in November this immature bird turned up in the Severn valley just yards from my garden. I was walking through the bushes alongside the river and could not fail to see it perched on the hogweed. I have found unusual birds before and seen hundreds of Shrikes but I still felt excited. Records of birds this late in the year are uncommon and in land-locked Montgomeryshire they are unheard of. I watched the bird for two hours that day before it dropped from sight and disappeared. One second it was in view through the telescope, the next it was not.

The following morning I walked the same path from the garden to the river that I have most days. There was no Shrike on the hogweed or the bushes. It was probably miles away. It had gone as it came – unnoticed.

Waxwings

I remember, when I was a child, looking through my first bird book and seeing illustrations of Waxwings. I thought I've got to see one of those.

The trouble was that Waxwings occured on the east coast and I lived in Hampshire. Clearly this was going to be a problem and was something to be taken seriously.

And so my quest began with visits to Norfolk in 1979. For successive winters I looked in gardens here and I looked in parks there but to no avail. I stayed in a bed and breakfast where an old lady insisted on telling me how she watched a group of six "funny-looking pink birds with crests" from her kitchen window only one week earlier. I nearly choked on my toast and marmalade. "I think they were called Waxwings", she said.

I muttered something about artists and pain. More near misses and no Waxwings later, I was taken to an estate in Sheringham and shown a cotoneaster bush stripped of berries by "funny-looking pink birds with crests". I had missed them by half an hour. I could take no more and retired wounded from Waxwing hunting.

Then in the winter of 1988/89 an invasion of Waxwings entered Britain from Scandinavia and Siberia, and groups of birds two hundred strong were recorded on the east coast. Something stirred inside.

I was now living in Wales and I asked myself could I justify dropping everything and driving 250 miles to fulfil a childhood dream? I convinced myself that there was no hurry and I would go for a long weekend trip as planned, in a couple of weeks time.

And then it happened. With so many Waxwings in the country, birds had dispersed and moved further west with some flocks reaching Wales. One telephone call to the RSPB office in Newtown was all it needed. A woman in Tregynon had seen some "funny-looking pink birds with crests" and fifteen minutes later I was watching Waxwings in a housing estate just five miles from my house. They were beautiful and they were magical and I remember doing the dance of the lost and found Waxwings. Of course, having seen Waxwings once, there is never a problem finding Waxwings again. They will turn up in the most suburban of places, and I have now seen them in supermarket car parks; the central reservation of dual carriageways and in a garden overlooked by ladies at their coffee morning. The setting never diminishes the spectacle though. Waxwings remain one of the most stunning of birds I have ever seen; an inspiration with their quiffs, their rouge and their painted wings. They are not at all funny-looking pink birds with crests.

Swans

At Aberhafesp the Severn valley plays host to a wintering flock of Whooper Swans. They arrive sometime in November or December and by the end of the year their numbers peak at a modest two or three dozen. Exactly where they come from I an unsure, but they are probably Russian birds from the Siberian Arctic. Every year their arrival prompts me to ponder the mystery of long distance migration, but perhaps as big a riddle is why they choose Aberhafesp as their winter quarters.

Hooper Swans — Aberhafesp

Fieldfare

Of Gulls and Crows

A gallery owner once told me not to paint Gulls. I thought this a somewhat strange suggestion. I paint Gulls because I enjoy watching them. Using live models as much as possible leads me often to look at familiar, more accessible birds, and Gulls are certainly familiar and accessible. In full adult plumage I would even venture that they are handsome with their pure whites and delicate shades of grey. No justification is ever needed for a painting that is faithfully observed, and if Gulls are deemed unpopular then it is perhaps more a comment on the tastes of picture buyers than on the merits of a work of art. The immature bird shown here is a Glaucous Gull that wintered on the Dyfi estuary at Ynys Hir.

Similarly another family of birds which is not often painted is Crows. Magpies are unpopular but I never tire of watching them. They can show brilliant blues and greens as well as striking patterns of white.

The First Snow

Most winters since my first in Wales in 1986/87 have been mild affairs. However before the year's end a rogue snow flurry will usually get me reaching for my gloves. After one such fall I went to Aberhafesp to look at the Whooper Swan flock and this was the scene.

While I watched I thought it interesting to note that the Swans appeared whiter than the snow. There were sheep in the field also and they typically looked dirty in the fresh snow. But the bodies of the Whoopers, save for their stained necks, were the brightest tone in the picture. The first snowfall was hardly enough to cover the field and it had accumulated only in the furrows. Through the telescope the foreshortening optical effect caused the horizontals to stack up instead of receding. I painted what I saw.

Kites

Before I lived in Wales I used to visit the hills and valleys of that country annually to see the upland species that were absent from my native Hampshire. A small group of us came every year in search of Dippers, Black Grouse, Peregrines and of course Red Kites. Of all the birds we wanted to see it was the Kite that filled the car with expectation and I remember particularly our first encounter. At the first glimpse of a forked tail the car slammed to a halt and the doors shot open. Anyone who remembers Ford Anglias will recall that they had only two doors, and I was in the back. How I managed to get out before the driver is mystery but I did, and my lasting memory is of my friend Paul being wedged between the tilted seat and steering wheel mumbling "Is it still there?" The impatience of youth.

In recent years there has been an attempt to reintroduce Kites into England and Scotland, and now sighting of individuals far from release sites are recorded in many counties. That fact not withstanding, the Red Kite for most people remains an essentially Welsh bird. Their hunting ground is the wild and lonely Cambrian plateau, and their breeding territories the wooded valleys that dissect this ancient land.

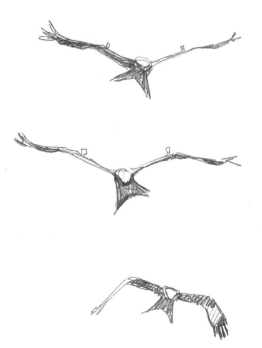

Blue Kites

For most of the year Kites are solitary in their habits, drifting across empty uplands in search of food, but in winter they gather in communal roosts and this can be a good opportunity to see many birds at once. Numbers vary from year to year, and indeed week to week, and the factors dictating the size of roost are not fully understood. However, when the temperature drops counts of forty birds are not uncommon, and it was on such an occasion that I witnessed the scene here. I was at Cwmystwyth waiting for the end of the day. There had been several Kites in the area for an hour before dusk, and then small groups moved in from further down the valley. They came across a "Peter Scott" sky in singles, pairs and in groups of threes and fours. Thirty-seven cool silhouettes sailing across the pink.